CHAMPLAIN

CHAMPLAIN

CHRISTOPHER MOORE

With archival artwork, maps, and artifacts

Additional illustrations by Francis Back

Tundra Books

This is a revised and expanded version of the book *Samuel de Champlain*, first published by Grolier in 1986.

Published in Canada by Tundra Books,
481 University Avenue, Toronto, Ontario M5G 2E9

Published in the United States by Tundra Books of Northern New York,
P.O. Box 1030, Plattsburgh, New York 12901

Library of Congress Control Number: 2004102430

National Library of Canada Cataloguing in Publication

Moore, Christopher, 1950–

    Champlain / Christopher Moore ; illustrated by Francis Back.

Originally published: Toronto : Grolier, 1986, under title: Samuel de Champlain
Includes bibliographical references and index.
ISBN 0-88776-657-9

1. Champlain, Samuel de, 1567–1635 – Juvenile literature. 2. New France – Discovery and exploration – Juvenile literature. 3. Canada – History – To 1663 (New France) – Juvenile literature. 4. Explorers – France – Biography – Juvenile literature. 5. Explorers – Canada – Biography – Juvenile literature. I. Back, Francis II. Moore, Christopher, 1950 –   . Samuel de Champlain. III. Title.

FC332.M65 2004   j971.01'13'092   C2004-901317-3

We acknowledge the financial support of the Government of Canada through the Book Publishing Industry Development Program (BPIDP) and that of the Government of Ontario through the Ontario Media Development Corporation's Ontario Book Initiative. We further acknowledge the support of the Canada Council for the Arts and the Ontario Arts Council for our publishing program.

Design: Terri Nimmo

Printed in Hong Kong, China

1 2 3 4 5 6   09 08 07 06 05 04

CONTENTS

New France is a new world, not simply a kingdom, beautiful in all perfection. . . . Consider the happiness people may one day have by inhabiting this country peaceably, free to live as they please.

– SAMUEL DE CHAMPLAIN

FOREWORD

ne July day four hundred years ago, Samuel de Champlain stepped out of a small boat at Québec and began a great adventure.

Champlain lived to travel and explore. He had fought in wars while he was still a teenager, had visited foreign lands and crossed the oceans. Several times he had been to Canada with the French traders and explorers who visited there each summer. He had also spent winters in Canada, even though at that time most Europeans made quick visits in the summer and fled home before the cold weather closed in.

This time, July 1608, the young explorer had come to stay. Champlain meant to build a permanent community, the first his people had ever attempted in Canada. It was a bold and dangerous venture he had been preparing for all his life. The rest of his days would be shaped by the community he would found: New France. They would be shaped even more by the great encounter between Europeans and First Nations in the land that is now Canada.

Even before Samuel de Champlain was born, generations
of European sailors had been crossing the Atlantic to fish,
to hunt whales, and to trade along the shores of what is
now Canada. In small wooden sailing craft, with simple
navigational tools and little protection against waves, ice,
storms, and accidents, they began to bind the continents
of Europe and North America together.

THE EARLY YEARS

he young man who loved adventure was born in a small and out-of-the-way town called Brouage, on the coast of France. No one there would have guessed that young Samuel de Champlain would grow up to be one of the great men of his time. In those days, the leaders of important events were lords and ladies favoured by the king of France. The Champlains of Brouage were neither rich nor famous.

All the same, Brouage was a good place for a boy who daydreamed of travel and adventure. The town was small, but it was a seaport, and Champlain's father and uncle were both sea captains. From them, and from the other sailors who went in and out of Brouage harbour, Champlain must have heard of bold explorers in strange foreign lands. The ocean that lay at his door had become a great highway to the wide world and all its dangers and adventures.

Less than one hundred years before Champlain was born, Christopher Columbus had sailed across the Atlantic and discovered America. Not long afterwards, John Cabot had sailed from England to explore the east coast of Canada. Then Jacques Cartier from France had travelled far up the St. Lawrence River. Suddenly sailors from towns like Brouage were roaming the world – and coming back rich with treasures and rich with stories.

CHAMPLAIN'S ASTROLABE

More than one hundred years ago, this astrolabe was found in the woods near the Ottawa River. Many people believe it was lost there by Samuel de Champlain.

Champlain used his astrolabe and a compass to help him find his way across the ocean and along the lakes and rivers of Canada. By observing the sun or the North Star through the sights on the arm of the astrolabe, he could see how far north he was. The compass showed the direction he was headed. Only by making these measurements very carefully throughout his journey could he draw accurate maps of the places he explored.

By the time Champlain was born, perhaps about 1580, the king of Spain ruled a great empire in Mexico and South America. France had no empire then and was at war. Champlain was just a teenager when he went to serve, and he fought in the wars for several years, until peace finally came to France in 1598.

At last Champlain could begin exploring the world. As soon as he could, he went to Spain. "My idea was to learn as much as I could and then enter the service of the King of France," he wrote. Because Spain had more sailors and ships than any other country, it was the best place for an adventurous youth. Soon Champlain found himself on a Spanish ship bound for the Caribbean islands and Spain's American conquests, which were called New Spain. He may even have travelled on to Mexico and seen the magnificent palaces and temples and other amazing sights there. But many historians believe the book that describes Champlain's experiences in New Spain was not really written by him and includes things he never saw. They doubt that he actually got as far as Mexico, and Champlain never mentioned it in anything else he wrote.

Almost two years passed before the young adventurer returned to France. Would anyone there have work for a bold young man who was now an experienced sailor and traveller? Yes, they would. In the summer of 1603, a fur-trading merchant agreed to take Champlain with him on a summer voyage to Canada.

Champlain wrote a book of his own about the things he saw in Canada that summer. He wrote about the great St. Lawrence River, and the way the Native peoples travelled easily along it. At Tadoussac, he saw a fleet of two hundred canoes, each one paddled by just two people, yet all going much faster than the ship's boat he was in. He described the great councils where the First Nations met, and how they traded furs with the visitors from France. He kept notes and drew maps of every part of the land he had seen. "You could hardly hope to find a more beautiful country," he wrote happily after he returned to France that fall.

Champlain now knew a little about the coasts of Canada, but almost nothing of what lay farther inland. He had travelled to Canada like an astronaut visiting a distant planet, marvelling at the wonders there. Already he wanted to go back. Canada promised adventure.

The inlet at Port Royal, now Annapolis Basin, Nova Scotia, is a long, deep harbour with a single narrow entrance from the Bay of Fundy. Not far from the entrance, Pierre de Monts's men, who included Samuel de Champlain and a young black interpreter named Mathieu da Costa, built the cluster of buildings that would be their home for three years.

FIRST ATTEMPTS AT SETTLEMENT

For years, French traders had been making summertime visits to Canada. Now there were Frenchmen who wanted to build a permanent fur-trading settlement there. Henri IV, the king of France, supported them. He hoped they would build a colony called New France. Perhaps one day it would be as great and valuable as the New Spain that Champlain had seen.

This was an adventure Champlain could not resist. His skill in drawing maps made him useful to the leaders of the expedition, and by the time the ships set sail in the spring of 1604, the commander, Pierre de Monts, had agreed to take young Champlain along as his cartographer.

The expedition leaders had decided to start their colony on the Atlantic coast of Canada, in the land they called Acadia, the home of the Mi'kmaq, Malecite, and Abenaki Native nations. In their first winter, the settlers huddled in temporary shelters on Ile Ste-Croix, near the head of the Bay of Fundy. They were not well prepared for the ferocious cold, and nearly everyone became ill. The next summer, they moved across the Bay of Fundy to Port Royal, where they built a

snug cluster of buildings around a courtyard beside a deep and sheltered harbour. Port Royal became the centre of the colony in Acadia for several years.

Champlain was kept busy exploring this rugged land. He searched for safe harbours, for rivers that led inland, and for valuable minerals and farmlands. He talked with Mi'kmaq leaders and traders, and he drew maps and wrote about his travels. Soon Champlain knew as much about the Atlantic coast of this new land as almost anyone

from Europe. Everyone agreed that his maps of Acadia were the best they had ever seen. Meanwhile, the leaders of the expedition worked to build a profitable trade in furs with the Native nations of Atlantic Canada. But the competition was fierce, and rival traders who came over from Europe each summer were not burdened with the costs of maintaining a colony.

By the colonists' third winter in Acadia, hunting, fishing, and trade with the Mi'kmaq people provided them with a lot of food, but the long,

PORT ROYAL AND THE ACADIANS

When he began his colony in Acadia in 1604, Pierre de Monts hoped that the climate along the seacoast would be milder than that inland at Québec. But he soon found that on the coast, he could not control the trade in furs. Despite all the money de Monts spent on the settlement, any rival trader could drop anchor in the next harbour down the shore and compete for business. At Québec, however, a single post would be able to control all the furs that came down the river from the interior. So de Monts's colonists abandoned Port Royal in 1607, and in 1608 Champlain led a new colony-building venture to the St. Lawrence.

While Champlain's Québec colony grew, other adventurers came to Acadia and built new forts and settlements along the coast from Cape Breton Island to the Saint John River. They soon returned to Port Royal as well. Although it was often attacked by rival traders and English raiders, the spacious, sheltered harbour on the Bay of Fundy kept attracting settlers.

In 1636, just after Champlain died, a fur-trading adventurer named Charles Menou d'Aulnay brought several families to Port Royal from his home region on France's west coast (not far from Champlain's birthplace, Brouage). These settler families soon began building dikes and draining the salt marshes at the head of the bay for pasture land. D'Aulnay drowned at Port Royal in 1650, but the settlers and their descendants spread out to develop new farming communities around the Bay of Fundy. They became the Acadians, the French-speaking people of Atlantic Canada.

THE ORDER OF GOOD CHEER

When winter came, how would a small band of pioneers spend their time? Samuel de Champlain had an idea. In 1606, he invented the Order of Good Cheer. Each day, one member of the order became "governor." He would provide all the others with something special for breakfast and dinner that day.

It became a competition. Before his turn came, each man went out to find tasty things to serve his friends. The members of the order ate mallards, geese, and partridges, and they tried the meat of otters, lynxes, bears, and rabbits. By spring, they had decided that the most delicious foods were beaver tails, moose pie, and sturgeon. Nothing in the kitchens of Paris seemed better than these.

Whatever the special treat was, there was always a ceremony to accompany it. When dinner was ready, the governor of the feast led the way, with a napkin on his shoulder, a staff in his hand, and the badge of the order around his neck. Everyone else paraded in behind him. After dinner, they gave thanks. Then the governor would present the badge of the order to the next day's governor, and they would all drink toasts to one another.

Champlain enjoyed being part of his Order of Good Cheer. He said it was better than medicine for keeping the men happy and healthy.

FRANÇOIS GRAVÉ DU PONT

No one sent ships across the ocean to Canada just for adventure. Merchants and traders paid for the vessels and crew that made Samuel de Champlain's early voyages possible. François Gravé Du Pont was one of these practical businessmen. Each year he loaded a ship with iron axes, copper kettles, cloth, and food. The First Nations of Canada liked his goods. They paid for them with beaver skins, and Gravé took the skins back to hatmakers and furriers in France. For many years, the trade in furs was the one great industry that made the exploration of Canada possible.

François Gravé soon saw that young Samuel de Champlain was brave, intelligent, and adventurous. He often helped Champlain learn more about Canada through his contacts with French and Native traders. When Champlain began his colony at Québec, Gravé visited him there nearly every year. He gave good advice to his young friend, and Champlain said, "I respect him like a father."

cold winters, when scurvy attacked and only the strongest survived, were still hard to endure. To keep up the spirits of his companions, Champlain started the Ordre de Bon Temps, the Order of Good Cheer. It kept everyone busy, and the long winter passed quickly.

In the spring of 1607, Champlain learned that the leaders had ordered that the expedition return to France. The traders were discouraged by the cost of the colony and the slow growth of the fur trade. The settlement in Acadia seemed a failure. After three years of effort, everyone went home.

Champlain, however, had proven himself. He was an expert sailor, traveller, and mapmaker who knew how to live in Canada's harsh conditions. He was growing into a leader. Perhaps he would succeed where others had failed, creating a thriving colony for France in the New World. Samuel de Champlain was ready for his greatest adventure.

Montagnais, Algonquin, Ottawa, and Ojibwa understood that
the way to thrive in the Canadian woodlands was to get by
with little. Their shelters, canoes, tools, and weapons were
brilliantly suited to the conditions in which they lived. But
their most precious possessions were in their heads: the skills
to produce the things and the foods they needed from the
environment around them.

CANADA IN 1608

he people of the First Nations in the lands Samuel de Champlain hoped to explore were also travellers and explorers. Around the time Champlain was becoming a leader among the French visitors to Canada, a man named Atironta was growing into a leader of his people, the Huron. Atironta wrote no books, and his maps were kept in his head or scratched on pieces of birchbark. But as Europeans and First Nations came into more constant contact in Canada, Atironta's life and Champlain's would become tangled together.

Atironta's people, perhaps thirty thousand strong, lived on pleasant rolling country between the lakes we now call Huron and Simcoe. These people had built a union of five nations whose names are beautiful but not easy to pronounce: Arendarhonon, Attignawantan, Attigneenongnahac, Tahontaenrat, and Tionnontaté. Together they formed a confederacy they called the Wendat, though it became better known by a name the French gave it, the Huron.

There were about twenty large towns in Huronia, some with as many as a thousand people in them. Each town was crowded with large wooden longhouses and fenced in against enemies by tall wooden palisades, or stakes.

What made the Huron confederacy so powerful were its farms, for the Huron were a farming people. They grew corn, beans, and squash in broad fields around their towns. These bountiful crops fed their large, settled population and also gave them something to trade with the hunting-and-gathering people who lived around them.

Atironta was a member of the Arendarhonon nation of the Huron confederacy. The Arendarhonon lived at the northern edge of the Huron country, and they handled much of the confederacy's trade. Trading parties set out from their towns each year to take foodstuffs to the hunting nations, so Atironta, like Champlain, grew up making long and sometimes dangerous voyages. He learned the trading languages that the different Native nations of the Great Lakes region used, and all the lake and river routes they relied on.

When Atironta's trading parties travelled north to the Ojibwa and Cree territory towards Hudson Bay, they brought back furs, or birchbark canoes, or flints. When they travelled east, they came to the territories of the Algonquin along the Ottawa River and the Montagnais farther away, along the St. Lawrence. From them, Huron traders got strange new European goods: kettles, blankets, and bits of metal, glass, and beads for decoration.

Sometimes Atironta travelled as a warrior, not as a trader. South of Lake Ontario lived the people who called themselves Hodenosaunee, meaning "the people of the longhouse." Their rivals called them Iroquois. They too were farmers, but that made them

ATIRONTA

It was a dangerous time for the Huron people. They were at war with the Iroquois nation, and it was not safe to trade or travel. When Atironta, one of the Huron chiefs, learned that a few Frenchmen were living at Québec, he decided to travel there and see for himself. Perhaps these newcomers would be able to help his people.

Atironta met Samuel de Champlain near Québec and was impressed. The newcomers had built a strong fort. They had many iron tools. Their guns and armour pleased the Huron chief. Atironta talked and feasted with Champlain, and soon they agreed to fight the Iroquois together and to trade with each other.

Atironta and Champlain were allied for years. They travelled together and shared many hardships. Atironta found that the French settlers were very different from his own people, but he respected Samuel de Champlain as a brave leader. And Champlain knew that New France would not have survived without the trade and support of Atironta's Huron confederacy.

competitors in trade, and not friends, of the Huron. Each feared that the other side might take control of the routes down to the coast, where the European traders were visiting. Even on trading voyages, Atironta and his comrades were armed and alert, for it grew more dangerous every year to travel towards the coast. Huron war leaders like Atironta were increasingly concerned about their nation's strength and about its trading partnerships. They were looking for new allies when Samuel de Champlain returned to Canada.

THE STRUGGLE TO BUILD NEW FRANCE

Champlain came back to Canada in 1608, and this time he was a leader, not a follower. He had helped persuade the king and some of the fur-trade merchants to start a colony at Québec, a site he had admired during his voyage up the St. Lawrence in 1603. Champlain would command the small band of men who would build a settlement and spend the first winter there.

In the language of the Montagnais people, Québec means "the place where the river narrows." Champlain was sure the rivers of Canada would lead him far into the unexplored land. Perhaps he would even find a way to the Western Ocean and the riches of China. The country upriver from Québec was also a rich fur-trading territory. If he could win the trust of the inland nations of Canada, Champlain could make Québec the gateway for the fur trade. Then New France could prosper and grow.

When Jacques Cartier visited Québec, back in 1535, there was a town called Stadacona at the place where the river narrows. But Stadacona had vanished, destroyed by wars and

(opposite) The artist has imagined Champlain in the elegant dress of a leader and commander as he supervises construction of the Habitation at Québec. But he was tough as well. When a mutiny broke out among the workers, Champlain had the ringleader executed and then displayed his head at the gate of his new building.

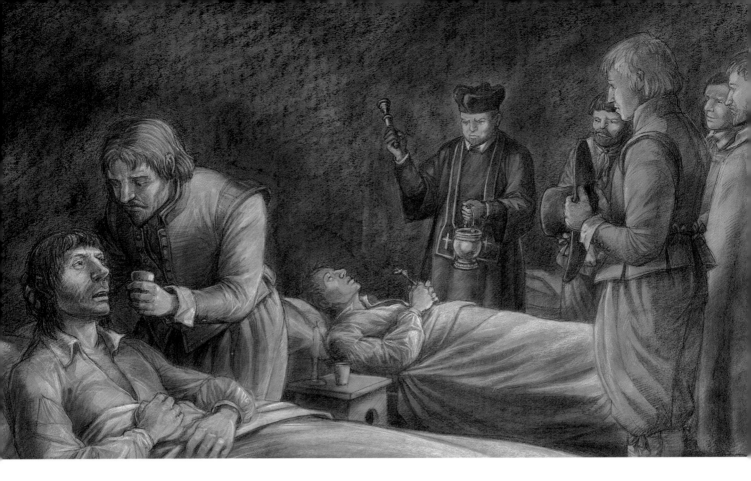

epidemics. In 1608, few people lived there. The Montagnais people, whose land it was, were willing to allow their French allies to settle there, for they wanted help protecting their trade along and travel on the river. So on July 3, 1608, at the foot of the great rock called Cape Diamond, Champlain and his workers began to build the "Habitation" where they would spend the winter.

Champlain hoped that his Habitation would be a snug and safe haven during the harsh Canadian winter. But he could not save his men from illness. The season was long and cold, there was no fresh food, and Champlain's men began to sicken and die of scurvy. Twenty-seven brave men had agreed to stay with him at Québec that first winter. In the spring, when the ice melted in the river and their friends returned from France, only eight men were still alive at the Habitation.

Champlain knew that his little colony was still in great danger. Very few Native traders had brought furs

ABITATION. DE QVEBECQ.

THE HABITATION

The drawing at left, first published in one of Champlain's books about his voyages, is his own sketch of the Habitation, his first home at Québec. The Habitation looked more like a fort than a village. There were just four small buildings, all enclosed with a high wall. Outside the wall were a deep ditch and a wooden fence. Inside the Habitation, Champlain and his men built the bedrooms and kitchen where they would sleep and eat, and the storerooms and workshops where they would keep busy in the winter.

When the Habitation was complete, Champlain proudly raised the flag of the king of France. He was sure that this tiny fort was going to be the beginning of a great colony.

The settlers at Québec eventually replaced this first Habitation with a stone fort on the same site. Today the historic Lower Town of Québec City covers the spot where the first Habitation once stood.

to Québec, and his small and sickly group could do nothing alone. Unless Champlain got the help of Native nations in the land to the west, his settlement would wither away. The other French traders, the ones who came to Canada only in the summer, might be glad to see the end of the new competitor. But Champlain's ambition to found a great colony would be ruined. Could New France survive?

Trade was not just business; it meant alliances, partnerships,
friendships, and trust. Holding up a trade item meant
offering a gift as proof of friendship. If the friendship was
accepted, the recipient would give gifts of equal worth.

ALLIANCES AND EXPLORATIONS

uring his explorations in 1609, Champlain travelled with a gun in his hand. The struggle among the Native nations to control the St. Lawrence River and the trade in furs made it impossible for trade canoes to travel safely on the rivers. That was why few traders had come down to Champlain's Habitation at Québec. Until the war was settled, they would not come. To build his colony, Champlain had to become a soldier and a traveller again.

In June 1609, Champlain hosted a great council. His guests were not traders but warriors, men like Atironta, "who knew how to fight and were full of courage, and who knew the country and the rivers." They had learned that the French traders who had settled at Québec the year before might help them in their war against the Iroquois. Some who came were Montagnais from the north shore of the St. Lawrence River. Others were Algonquin from the Ottawa River country; they came with their leader, Iroquet. The Huron, who lived far away on the shores of Lake Huron and had never met Frenchmen before, also made the journey.

There was feasting and dancing around Champlain's rough Habitation beneath the cliffs of Québec. The French, the Montagnais, the Algonquin, and the Huron exchanged

Champlain and his arquebus are clearly visible in the centre of this illustration of his 1609 battle with the Iroquois. The illustration was published in the book he wrote about those events, but it was not drawn by him, and the artist imagined many of the details.

gifts and made speeches of friendship. They agreed on a great alliance. Champlain would go with them to make war on their common enemy.

Soon Champlain, two French companions, and the First Nations warriors were travelling together in canoes into the disputed grounds south of the St. Lawrence River. They met their enemy by the edge of a lake.

"The Iroquois came slowly to meet us with a gravity and calm which I admired," wrote Champlain. He was determined to show his allies he could be useful to them, so from the midst of his army, he stepped forward and strode towards the three enemy leaders. The Iroquois had never seen anything like this: a man wearing metal armour and a helmet, carrying a gun called an

THE CANOE

Samuel de Champlain had sailing ships to carry him across the Atlantic, but once he reached Canada, he found that he could travel much farther in the boat that the peoples of Canada used: the canoe.

The First Nations made their canoes of birchbark. They peeled long, wide pieces of bark from living trees and attached them to a light wooden frame. These canoes were strong enough to ride the white water of river rapids, yet they were so light that it was simple to carry them past waterfalls.

Canoes were perfect for the Canadian rivers. They could go anywhere, could carry a lot, and were easy to make and repair. Champlain's people had only one complaint: when they were passengers in the canoes, they had to crouch motionless for hours, and so they got stiff and sore.

In the summer of 1611, Champlain put his life in the hands of his Native allies when he "rode the rapids" of the St. Lawrence River in a canoe. It was a demonstration of both his trust and his courage, for Champlain did not know how to swim.

arquebus. They fired arrows at him, but Champlain came closer. He aimed his gun, fired, and the three Iroquois leaders fell dead. Champlain's French companions also began to fire their guns, and the Iroquois fighters, who had never had to face such weapons before, retreated. Champlain and his friends had won a victory, and they made it look easy to their Native allies.

From that day, Champlain's people were part of the war that pitted the Huron and the other northern nations against the Iroquois nation to the south. The Huron and their French allies could not defeat the powerful Iroquois, who quickly learned how to fight men with guns and soon acquired guns of their own, but travel on the St. Lawrence gradually became safer. Soon the Habitation at Québec was busy, as Huron, Ottawa, Algonquin, and others exchanged their furs for the axes, blankets, kettles, food, and beads the French traders brought from Europe. The French settlement was

THE FUR TRADE

A Montagnais leader who came to trade with Champlain's people made a joke about the beaver. "The beaver does everything perfectly," he said. "It makes kettles, hatchets, swords, knives, and bread. It makes everything."

Of course beavers do not make things. He meant that if he brought beaver skins to the French traders, they would give him the kettles and hatchets and other goods that his people had never had before.

Why did the French traders want beaver skins? It was mainly because the men of Europe liked to wear hats. Hatmakers would shave the soft, fine hair from the beaver skins. These hairs have thousands of tiny rough barbs that help to trap air and keep a swimming beaver warm. Because of these rough edges, the hairs shaved from a beaver skin stick to each other. By crushing the hairs together, hatmakers could make an excellent soft felt hat.

Hatmaking was a big business, and thousands of beaver furs were required every year to supply its needs. For 250 years, the fur traders and the peoples of Canada exchanged kettles, weapons, cloth, and food for beaver skins so that European men could wear hats made of beaver-fur felt.

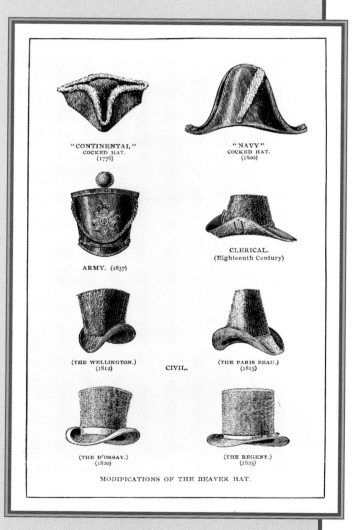

"CONTINENTAL," COCKED HAT. (1776)

"NAVY" COCKED HAT. (1800)

ARMY. (1837)

CLERICAL. (Eighteenth Century)

(THE WELLINGTON.) (1812)

CIVIL.

(THE PARIS BEAU.) (1815)

(THE D'ORSAY.) (1820)

(THE REGENT.) (1825)

MODIFICATIONS OF THE BEAVER HAT.

safe, and Atironta's warriors and traders became frequent visitors.

Now Champlain began to do what he was most proud of doing: going into unknown places to discover things Europeans had never seen. Ever since his first visit to Canada, Champlain had been asking his Native allies all about their country. He now saw the great rivers and lakes for himself, and he admired the country more than ever.

In 1615, after several summers of exploration, the Huron took Champlain on the longest of his voyages. At last they would bring him along the Ottawa River route to the faraway land of the Huron nation. Day after day, Champlain and the others paddled across lakes and along rivers. They portaged their canoes and goods past waterfalls and rapids, and they slept under the trees each night. No European had ever been so far inland in Canada. As he advanced up the Ottawa River, Champlain thought he had never seen such wild country. It seemed to him rugged, barren, and barely inhabited. For nearly a month, the canoe voyage continued.

Then the travellers reached Lake Huron. Champlain called it the Mer Douce, the "freshwater ocean." His Huron guides and companions led the way along the shore of this inland sea, and soon they reached the land of the Huron. "Here we found a great change in the country, this part being very fine," Champlain noted.

He spent nearly a year with his Huron allies, travelling with Atironta and other warriors to attack Iroquois towns, taking part in deer hunts, and visiting many Huron villages. Once he became lost in the woods and nearly starved. Once he was wounded by an Iroquois arrow, and his Huron companions had to carry him to safety on their backs.

Living among the Huron people, Champlain learned about their customs. "The women," he wrote, "have almost the whole care of the house and the work. They till the soil, sow the corn, lay up wood for the winter, strip the hemp and spin it, and with the thread make fishing nets for catching fish. They harvest their corn, store it, prepare it for food, and attend to the household." Although the men traded, built the houses, hunted, and fought in the wars, Champlain thought their lives

were easier. "On their return, they do not stir from the feasts and dances," he observed.

In his books, Champlain tried to describe the Huron way of life, but it was always strange to him. He needed the support of Huron traders and soldiers, but he never really understood them. He was eager to return to his own people, and though he hoped that French missionaries would convert the Huron to his religion, he preferred to live in the French colony at Québec.

After his winter in Huronia, Champlain travelled back to his Habitation, and his friends there celebrated his return from the far west. He had not discovered the Western Ocean or the route to China, and he never would. But he had seen a country unknown to Europeans and filled with strange and fascinating things. He had travelled the shores of lakes as large as seas and met Native peoples who lived in fortified towns surrounded by abundant fields of corn.

Trade in fish and furs paid for European dreams of colonies
and empires in North America. The artist here imagines a
richly dressed Champlain impressing a cluster of half-dressed
nomads with a lavish display of luxuries and tools. But
humble beaver pelts fuelled most of the trade in Canada,
and Native trappers were the ones who supplied those to
the eager newcomers.

A Thriving Settlement

The little Habitation at Québec had grown stronger while Champlain was away exploring. Each year, his men learned more from their Native allies, and that made it easier to spend a safe and healthy winter there. Each summer, the Huron and the other Native traders came to talk and to trade. For the merchants back in France, Québec was already a success.

But would New France just be a place where a few men exchanged goods for furs with the First Nations traders? Samuel de Champlain dreamed of a great colony. He wanted families to settle there, not just workmen. He wanted Québec to be a real town with houses and churches, and New France to be a growing colony with farming and fishing, as well as the trade in furs. Now Champlain encouraged other men to go exploring and travelling with the allies from the First Nations. He had promised the king that he would make him proud of his colony, so he stayed at Québec to lead his people.

Slowly, Champlain's dream began to come true. People in France had to admit that this stubborn man was succeeding.

ETIENNE BRÛLÉ

Etienne Brûlé loved the Canadian wilderness even more than Champlain did. In fact, he decided to live there all his life.

Brûlé was probably in his teens in 1610 when he and Champlain agreed that he would go with the First Nations and learn their languages. No Frenchman had ever gone to live among the faraway Huron before, and when Brûlé returned to Québec a year later, Champlain was amazed. The young Frenchman was dressed like his Native hosts, spoke their language, and was proud to be part of a Huron trading voyage.

Etienne Brûlé lived with the Huron for twenty years. He loved the free and simple life he found among the people who adopted him, and he travelled with them to places no other Frenchman had ever seen before – not even Samuel de Champlain.

Etienne Brûlé and Champlain both loved adventure, but while Champlain devoted himself to building New France, Brûlé chose the life of the First Nations who had always been there. Yet even he never entirely became one of them. In 1633, in the midst of great upheavals in the fur trade and the Huron alliances, he got into some unexplained dispute with his hosts and was killed.

They admired his books of adventure and the maps he drew, and they began to support his plans for New France. They began to believe that Champlain's colony was going to last.

In 1615, the first missionaries had come to Québec. One went to Huronia with Champlain that summer, for the missionaries were eager to convert the Native peoples to Christianity. Others stayed at Québec, building a residence and a chapel to serve the settlers there. Strengthening the Catholic faith among the settlers and bringing Christianity to the Natives were two ways Champlain hoped to reinforce New France and gain the aid of the Roman Catholic Church. From 1615 on, missionary priests, brothers, and nuns were an important part of Champlain's plans for building a great community.

Two years after the missionaries arrived, Louis Hébert brought his family to Québec. Until then, only single men, mostly sailors, traders, and working men, had lived at Champlain's Habitation. The Héberts were the first family to settle in New France, and the first settlers to take an interest in growing crops there. Others followed, trusting Champlain to keep them safe. Once Champlain had just been a young man seeking adventure. Now he was the chief of a growing community.

AFTER CHAMPLAIN

hamplain had always wanted to make New France precious and valuable to France. "These colonies, though at first of little account, nevertheless in the course of time will equal the states of the greatest kings," he once wrote. After his death, the colony on the St. Lawrence continued to grow. Soon there were a few hundred settlers, and then a few thousand, and many families began to farm the land surrounding the Habitation.

The trade in furs remained important to Champlain's people and to Atironta's. Atironta led many more trading voyages and many more war parties. The Huron people now had weapons, blankets, kettles, metal tools, and all the other goods the French traders had offered them. But they were still not safe. The war with the Iroquois went on, and there were other dangers.

The French always insisted that the Huron welcome the Catholic missionaries among them, even though most of the Huron preferred their own way of life and disliked being told that the Christian way was better. Worse, the French people living among the Huron could not help spreading sickness – illnesses that the Huron people had never known and against which they had no resistance. The closer the French and the Huron grew, the more frequently Huron men, women, and children died.

Some Huron began to argue that their confederacy should break its alliance with the French and make peace with the Iroquois. But one of Atironta's fellow leaders said sadly that if they tried to live two years without going to Québec to trade, the proud Huron would end up having to abandon their towns and fields of corn to live like the nomadic hunters to whom they had always felt superior.

The war went on. In the 1640s, the Huron confederacy was destroyed by it. Atironta was already dead, but two more young Huron in turn had taken

his name to honour his leadership and courage. One of them was killed fighting the Iroquois. The other became a refugee near Champlain's city of Québec.

Champlain's alliances with the First Nations of Canada had made it possible for his colony to gain a foothold. His settlers and traders learned how to survive in Canada from their Native allies, and it was Native trappers and traders who brought in the furs to keep the trading posts busy. All Champlain's maps and explorations depended on the guidance and information that First Nations explorers gave him. It would be that way throughout the European explorations of Canada. But the Huron were only one of many First Nations groups that suffered greatly in the exchange.

THE CHAMPLAIN MYSTERIES

How old was Champlain?

Historians used to believe that Champlain was born around 1567. If so, he would have been about thirty-six when he first came to North America and about sixty-eight when he died. Today, some historians believe that he was more likely born about 1580 and came to New France as a young man of twenty-three. Their evidence for the "younger" Champlain seems convincing, and we have followed it in this book. But no one knows Champlain's age for sure.

What did Champlain look like?

The most familiar "portrait" of Champlain, seen on page 45, does not portray him at all – it is a mislabelled painting of a French financier from the 1600s. No reliable portrait of Champlain is known to exist. In all of Champlain's writings, he never gave a clue to what he looked like.

Where is Champlain's grave?

Champlain was buried at the Notre-Dame church in Quebec in 1635, but that building burned down in 1640. Since then, many other buildings have covered the site. Archaeologists investigating Old Québec have searched for bones that might be the remains of Samuel de Champlain, but his precise resting place will probably remain unmarked forever.

HiSTORiC SiTES AND MONUMENTS

Samuel de Champlain travelled to many interesting places, and several of them now have statues or plaques that honour him. Look for them when you travel in Ontario, Québec, or the Maritime provinces of Canada.

Ontario

There is a statue of Champlain in Orillia, Ontario, near one of the places where he stayed with his Huron friends. Not far from there is Sainte-Marie-among-the-Hurons, where you can see how life was lived in Huronia. Farther north, at Samuel de Champlain Park near North Bay, you can still go canoeing on one of the wild rivers that he travelled more than 350 years ago. High above the Ottawa River, near Parliament Hill, stands another statue of Champlain.

Québec

Right at the heart of the Old City of Québec, on the top of the cliff above the site of his Habitation, there is a statue of Champlain overlooking the city he founded and the river he explored.

On the United States border south of Montreal is Lake Champlain, which Samuel de Champlain named after himself. By the shore of this lake, he fought his first battle against the Iroquois.

Nova Scotia

Near Annapolis Royal, you can visit the rebuilt Habitation of Port Royal and see how the explorers lived in Acadia during the years when Champlain and his companions created the Order of Good Cheer.

READING ABOUT CHAMPLAIN

One way to know Champlain's world is to read his books. Between 1922 and 1936, an organization called the Champlain Society published a complete set of all the books Champlain wrote, with the French text, an English translation, all of the original illustrations, and a lot of useful comments by the editor, H. P. Biggar. You can find Samuel de Champlain's *Works* through libraries, and you can also look at them online at the website of the Champlain Society Digital Collection, at http://eir.library.utoronto.ca/champlain/search.cfm.

Many biographies of Champlain have also been written. You may find ones by Morris Bishop, Joe C. W. Armstrong, and Samuel Eliot Morison still available in libraries.

The *Dictionary of Canadian Biography*, volume 1, has short pieces about Champlain and many of his contemporaries. The *Dictionary of Canadian Biography* is available in many libraries or online at http://www.biographi.ca/EN/, a site hosted by the National Archives of Canada and the National Library of Canada.

The *Historical Atlas of Canada*, volume 1 (Toronto: University of Toronto Press, 1987), has wonderful maps of early Canada at the time of Champlain.

Conrad Heidenreich's *Huronia* (Toronto: McClelland and Stewart, 1971) and Bruce Trigger's *Natives and Newcomers* (Montreal: McGill-Queen's University Press, 1986) are two thick books full of information from two expert Canadian scholars of the time in which Champlain lived.

To compare Champlain's adventures with those of Jacques Cartier, who explored Canada seventy-five years earlier, read *The Voyages of Jacques Cartier*, edited by Ramsay Cook (Toronto: University of Toronto Press, 1993).

Finally, you can read diaries and reports from many other explorers of Canada in *Canadian Exploration Literature: An Anthology*, edited by Germaine Warkentin (Toronto: Oxford University Press, 1994).

ACKNOWLEDGMENTS

Special thanks to:

- *Ken Pearson, who first got me thinking about Samuel de Champlain;*
- *Kathy Lowinger's Tundra team, who brought me back to him; and*
- *Kate and Elizabeth and their classmates and teachers at High Park Alternative School in Toronto, who kept me thinking about him in between.*

ILLUSTRATION CREDITS

54

INDEX